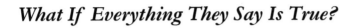

What If Everything They Say Is True?

What If Everything They Say Is True?

Christian Lindo

First Printing: 2018

ISBN 978-1-387-90967-4

Library of Congress Control Number: 2018910184

litotes 208
Ft. Lauderdale, Fl
info@litotes208.com

Design by Sonny Mangat -Designworx Media Group

For my sister, Stephanie

Everything considered,
a determined soul will always manage.
—-Albert Camus

You're here when you're here
—-John Lee Hooker

Poems

What If Everything They Say Is True?

Read Me As Though I Were A Posthumous Confession

Read me as though I were a posthumous confession
bringing forth the truths of some forgotten journey
like the simple description of a painting lost in a fire
give art to this life tethered to the burdens of our absolute

When the memories of your heart wake to find my verse
remind them how the fluidity of fate keeps everything above ground
nothing which touches the road avoids impermanence
save for the life breathed into me by your arousal

We Saw Her One Last Time In Town

She watched her skirt rest politely above her knees,
as she dug her toes into thick mud, which lay beneath the rich foliage.
To discern between land and form was an undertaking so
impotent she nearly gave the moment away to fruitless thought.
This sock of mud or root of flesh weathered by the act of living
was hers and hers alone. A variegated caryatid, unmoved by a steady
stare or a vacant witness, unswayed by some specious knowledge
passed from one man to another who ignored the fact that their words
could no longer capture the things she had to say. No menacing wind
nor threatening sky could provoke diversion from her state, for she
recognized that her gaze must remain unflinching.

The Heart Bayoneted, A Common Thing

We sang while swimming in tainted water

I thanked the heavens for your divine glow

As the erstwhile rivals remained on show

Attempting to lead us both to slaughter

As a common doubt turns peak to plateau

And our steady tread now turns a totter

A bygone agent becomes a plotter

To reveal to us what we both must know

The heart bayoneted, a common thing

Or the ruthless pain to which we both cling

Befouling the heart 'til it turns rotten

Before our singing becomes forgotten

Madrigal

Making an effort to breathe more clearly

I clutch at my chest to survey the waves

And conjure the tides, which my mind depraves

An empty vessel yearning sincerely

Or a thunderous force of hollowed caves

Making an effort to breathe more clearly

I clutch at my chest to survey the waves

An imposed belief to act austerely

With subtle commands, which feel more like raves

But a fill for the void is what it craves

Making an effort to breathe more clearly

I clutch at my chest to survey the waves

And conjure the tides, which my mind depraves

What Heights The Helmsman Loved

The turgid tides of love so thick

could swallow an ancient mariner's vessel.

But the wily captain would know every trick

for his heart may be stalked or sessile.

Shifting to another disguise

love made a change to the weather.

Lightning cracked as the captain surmised,

"The sky and sea must be working together."

Grabbing hold of the helm, heading straight to the port

The captain knew where he needed to be.

Through the thunder and rain, love made a retort

"I'm on land just as much as at sea."

The captain paused, turned his head to the sky

And said, "Fleeing's not why I head to the shore."

He was experiencing love, alone and awry.

He wanted time with his paramour.

A Phantom Thread

The devilish tangle of their sour hearts, with simple frames and tattered desires, requests the reassurance of unadorned acclaim

A simple turn of phrase, open to attack like a heart outside the chest, resembles the monster turning on its maker

But the thing remains the same

Each hand willingly rummaging through the other's remains, seeking the locus of those bygone cardial events, aflame with the desire to strangle their lover back to life

The Ancient Habit Sticks

The ramparts of Patagonia remained familiar, and so they clung to
them.
fearful of pilferers, fearful of barbarians

The autochthons hadn't been seen in years, but the inhabitants waited.
knowing of their time, knowing of their place

They were the natives now, yet they ignored how the land dismissed
their presence.
rejected by the soil, itself rejecting the earth's rotation

The children divorce themselves from the sentry, for they knew who
they were.
resentful of their prescription, envious of all other experiences

So the elders moved the boundaries, and the dwindling territory
became the symbol of an attack impending.
careful of their movements, circumspect in their suppression

With each wave of doubt, the elders moved the border, and the empire
turned to nothing.
obedient to their trepidation, acquiescent in their demise

Untitled

Another silent hour passes without her mercurial charge

Return and set me free to prowl the abundance of your landscape and stalk the sources of your flame

Avert your eyes away from the thing which captures your attention and press your stare against me as I seize the prey of your russet design

There will be no distinguished grace, no elemental impulse of felicity

Only the rapturous sounds of you seeing yourself in my reflection and me seeing mine in yours

Holed Up In An Ancient Colony

No Kingdom for those whose souls have been bared
Pensive reflection occurs at moonlight
Seraphs are swarming, but we are not spared

No matter the deed, they live their life scared
The heart is pumping though it stays contrite
No Kingdom for those whose souls have been bared

The anxiousness bubbles, scorn becomes flared
Reluctance transforms to feelings forthright
Seraphs are swarming, but we are not spared

Figures emerged, but there's no one who cared
Sable black pelts smother last whits of fight
No Kingdom for those whose souls have been bared

Naught from the space where allegiance declared
Few verities in a promised birthright
Seraphs are swarming, but we are not spared

A lifetime of lies left us unprepared
Few figures we see are gaily bedight
No Kingdom for those whose souls have been bared
Seraphs are swarming, but we are not spared

What Will We See If We Wait Long Enough?

Put it so;

What will we see if we wait long enough?

The dying embers of a love rebuffed

Or the prattle talk of a world so tough

Whose patron saints leave our hands in cuffs.

Put it so;

There is always an end to the applause

So silence reigns as the world withdraws

But keeps on turning for some noble cause

Though the constant movement causes constant pause.

Put it so;

We stay cemented in our own security

While bragging of one's own maturity

Fearful of some faint impurity

Which gifts us to the world's obscurity

Put it so;

What will we see if we wait long enough?

…

Something Else In Mind

The winter fowl thrusts itself about the snowy plain
recognizing it's the only way

Before its pension was raided by a wandering crane
sacrificing an impressive wealth to avoid delay

With the journey enough, it let others deign
they recognized the force and remained at bay

So the winter fowl thrashed across the blessed domain
creating a paradise in its own decay

The Agitated Princess

Like an agitated princess burning at the stake

whose tethered hands, with their arboreous branches,

cling to one another like some strange parasitic love affair.

Elevated to some spectacular height,

she sets her gaze upon the crowd. The men, whose posture

lets her know how they feel about the world, return her look

and slowly inch away as the raging flame sets about

the sweltry atmosphere.

There is no perfect setting, only cloudiness so considerable

that the men lose themselves in a sea of identical figures.

No longer dedicated to the mystery of the princess and the agitation

they named, the men hold on to one another like some strange

parasitic love affair. Only, they know not what they cling to. The

urgency of desire requires action, but the swelling smoke begins to

resemble the way the princess's dress billowed out around her, leaving

the men dependent on someone else.

The Proselytizers

When I allow them to evangelize, I open myself to the history of their predecessors. Clawing away at this pile of dirt I call my own, they linger, coercing me to claim the days ahead, with all this pain, as my own. Their hands, not around my throat, instead, politely resting on my lap, act as a reminder, or maybe a capable warning. I cannot say they fester because the only smell emanating from their presence is that of home. The subtle familiarity of gardenia-scented balm fused into my mother's skin. It is always there. They are always there, and their presence is not of my control. I witness kin stroll and withstand the pull while others plod under the weightiness of embers someone always says are dying. Though there remains some breath at the ready to fuel it for another lifetime.

Somewhere in between, I stand tethered to a thing so invisible those surrounding me ignore my descriptions. They can smell the gardenia too, but they misconstrue it as a comfort. Leaving them believing the worst about themselves. I implore them to engage, and worry that it is all for naught. So, I pensively dream of a time where the festering sores of my rotting flesh will emit a smell about their homes reminding them of my presence, and the work of those who evangelize.

A Striking Figure

I saw San-Souci, and that was the end of me.
The beings within took part in an exodus so quiet
there were no chances to ask for directions…
so I stood. Towering over me, but perfectly able to
live inside my pockets, I return her gaze and
see the bend in her back just below the spare curls, which
remind the men what lay beneath her tignon. A meticulous,
birdlike woman whose presence alone speaks the words
she desires for your ears. The weightiness of their imposition
modeled atop her frame like a oiseau, confident in its plume.
Closing my eyes, I allow her gaze to take hold. I sense the
beings return, but they are not the same. Now they are new,
and now they are dignified.

Dialogue Of A Love Once Young

Take me into your confidence

Allow me to see the world through your gaze

We'll struggle without consequence

And leave the world behind ablaze

Turn your back to that which holds you dear

Lead me through times the most severe

I see the misfortune you've failed to plan for

But I cannot save you without drowning myself

The pendulum's swung, we are bent and hoar

The times you speak of sit filed on a shelf

Together we envy the birds that have flown

But today we must sit tethered, alone

Standing Here I Am Very Far Away

I trundle towards you with wounded hands

Promising to meet all of your demands

But as I stand before you, you make no sound

So I stain your shirt clawing for commands

My soul, it sinks towards the ground

My breath abates as my claims resound

The journey here has left me weak

And your sightless stare chooses to confound

This humbled man has now turned meek

As my wounded heart begins to reek

The journey was questioned from the early start

But instead of havoc it is love I wreak

Face to face, but never more apart

Your statuesque stance like a work of art

I step away, but before I depart

I open my chest to give you my heart

I Walked On Mottled Ground

Today I watched as history began

from the white heat of a tremulous light.

Urged against a flaking bark,

I placed my feet upon boughs so withered and dry

they murmured like an old song.

I could not shuffle through the ragged wood

as the bark clung to me in wanton distress;

so, I closed my ears to sounds of forgetful sins

and set my mind upon the source before I understood

my eyes were all I had to see.

The house they share appeared in fullness

and towering behind it a pyramid of bones.

Their featureless figures and pulsating demeanor

struck me as familiar, but undesirable.

Was this the we to which I belong?

Rummaging through the pyramid, as bones trickled

down like pebbles. They gathered what they could and

attempted to place them in some particular order.

Helplessly, I watched as my restlessness went unnoticed,

or mistaken as an attempt to be free.

In the tree roots, which erupted through the path,

there were signs of movement once before,

like proof of an ocean's floor at low tide.

The resurrection of the half-formed things

failed and fell on a root's pointed prong.

Then a stillness arose as a puzzle began to take shape.

A figure of bones stood tall before blessing the landscape

with its initial steps. Like a griot eager to tell a tale,

it made its way down the path. Today I watched

as history began, but that history does not belong to me.

After That I Came Back To The World

To slumber by the river's edge

While a split of golden orioles

Nest atop the cottonwoods

Holding hands to make a pledge

We envy the desire they have

To make a place to call their own

The pomp is something we allege

And apply it to ourselves in case

We'd forgotten what we're supposed to be

So in our lives we force, we wedge

Misremembering times never there

With the hope they'll tell us where we're going

As we watch the birds from our ragged hedge

The dreams we have of joining the orioles

Remain a dream belied by a perfect slumber.

Renunciation

Sweetness burnt a hole in my tongue

and kept my eyes from seeing color.

Then the fount of understanding rung

as the clarion signaled the undiscovered.

What's new and old would sing, had sung

the simple phrases they'd always utter.

But like fog, the sweetened pain, it hung

and left me on my own to mutter.

Reclamation

We are the truth no one believes

from birth, they've fed us sour milk

ignoring our presence, our sobs, our heaves

and what they owe us they'll surely bilk

threaten to run though no one leaves

they may not be truth, but they're of our ilk

clenching their fists, for them we're thieves

as our years protect us like hardened silk

The Handle Toward My Hand

There is no dream within which we live,

only fugues of ill-mannered boasters

clamoring for moments of despair, so

they can talk their way through the lives of others.

There is no magic, only the magician

who helps us believe that those who disappear

will one day return in sequined gowns and black ties

even after we have cut them in two.

There is no death to speak to, only death to speak of

while some necromancer muddles our nature

by forcing us to preserve the moments where

lips and hands were used interchangeably.

There are no nightmares to keep us afraid,

for the terror-stricken are the magic which

they seek and the dream they had forgotten

long before they knew there was no thing.

A Paradise Beneath Their Detonated Vision

Consume my wound and make me whole

like the fabled balm of Gilead.

The ancient cry of "save my soul"

is lost amongst the myriad

of broken backs, and the strangled call

of men whose knees we hear as they buckle.

There are those who live with a sense so small

all is naught just as long as we truckle.

But the time has arrived for us to uncover

that we are for whom the bell will toll

what a miraculous day for them to discover

that we can make our own selves whole.

Between The Shore And Me

I have arrived to be forgotten
By bloated thoughts now seen as rotten.
To turn away from those besotten
I ignore that I'm the child begotten.

Under an isolated fog I hide
As the shadow it casts marks the rising tide.
Drowning in commands to which they abide
The others tread as they begin to chide.

With feet not buried, but resting on the shore
I hear some yell, while others just implore
I turn my ears to the assembled roar
As the howls transform to sounds I adore.

So I leave the shore for the final time
And find an empty space, which I now call mine.
I turn back to shore for those who remain divine.
As I begin to tread and make an endless climb.

What If Everything They Say Is True?

Today I found the seeds of hysteria blooming within me
and attempted to remind myself of the value of things being lost.
My failed efforts at reforming the garden where the seeds were
sown, where the fate of Adam and Eve was promised to them long
before they exchanged pleasantries, forced me to concede that this
is a place where wisdom is no more than a guess, only slightly
educated.

Thinking of traveled roads and trodden paths, I sweat while
traversing walls and climbing mountains. Clutching my bags whenever
I encounter another alpinist making their way towards where
I have just escaped. There is a self-imposed silence. I refuse to share
why I have chosen to relinquish my post, so it is only fair that I
make no effort to understand what antinomy may greet me ahead.

As the citizens choreograph themselves to ensure they die in
control of how they start the day, I ask myself, where was I during
some of those times? Using my feet to propel me from my morning
cup of coffee to a snack I sneak late at night after an initial jaunt
from a tranquil slumber, I do not return before I remind myself -
keep reminding myself - of the value of things being lost.

Everything depends upon places of failure highlighting the
places of strength, but a lifetime of waiting to do what we are meant
to do has left me unable to determine if my garden is the
paradisiacal Eden or the barren land of those who fell long before
I came into existence. So, I remain here in the hope that my lost
colony remains undiscovered, so the others can make of it what they
wish.

How It Sounds When Two Games Collide

Rub two sticks together and they will dance
as their malignant hearts succumb to the
buoyant solutions which keep them beating.
Where the sensitive malice of forethought
is no longer implied, or stated explicitly, rather
it hangs like a portrait constantly staring, but easily
ignored. This is the environment where acts,
premeditated and consciously crafted, dissipate
under the resonant sounds of stake on stake,
bone on bone, flesh on flesh. This is where the
human form, whether frozen in a statuesque stance
or dancing serpentinely, is used to repair the
breech of those who are honor bound to deceive.
It is here where the feeling that there is a nobility to the
human spirit exists as a perpetual epiphany. So, when
there is a need to travel they listen because they
know the words are just another kind of disguise.

How Close To Home Must We Get...

The agonizing sound of triumph rings about my ears like Caliban failing to capture a dream.

The bitterness slowly accumulates a height to match that of my companion.

I lie still wondering if our cars accurately count the miles or are they stealing their way into every man's dream.

The winters shorten, leaving less time for us to hibernate, forcing us to bath our Judas in fully bloomed bouquets of spring flowers.

I can hear her standing in the passageway. The presence, as faint as it may feel, interrupts the reminder that everything is temporary.

Our banality cannot be contained by the world, let alone this room, so we listen as the others sing our praises.

And as they do, I ask the question, to no one in particular: Does getting rid of everything truly lighten the load?

What We Assume We Can Get Away With

She realized one troubled day that she had never screamed
no matter how her path was blocked, or difficult life seemed
While others rant and rave, she responded with a stare
and thought of days she heard her voice, which was only when she
    dreamed.

The way someone projects is used to value how they care
but she knew the way she felt needed no buttress nor flare
For those who understood her ways, her support they didn't doubt
so their regard for her rapport was something they'd declare.

Then one day when life began she turned and looked about
In need of some support the ravers took another route
She called for their companionship, but found herself alone
She knew her whispered tones were drowned out by the way they
    shout.

Then she thought it might be time to manipulate her tone
To raise her voice and call for help like the others, be their clone
But when she made her mouth to shout she simply made a groan
For her shuttered calls and hushed notes were all she'd ever known.

When The Tilted Vision Descends Again

Today there will be no delicate caress
because years are moving faster than days,
yet they refuse to move aside for me.

We travel across the same bridge
as the spirit of protest lays dormant
and the young and old alike seek applause.
Everything we achieve is sadder than yesterday,
but tomorrow will be an exercise in anticipation.
Firmly rooted, we imagine that we are the trees
which purposefully drop our leaves
as our branches blot out our surroundings,
keeping our minds pale as if they never saw sunlight.

Bring forth a bounded spirit, so I may manage
the rasp I must surely endure when I step
away from this formerly forged path and
find myself barefoot in the bitterness of winter.

A Disorderly Place of Desirable Excesses

In quite a constant way, bygone memories return.
Outfitted as a destructive character and
occasionally, greeted welcomingly, the way cold hands
receive the warming of the sun, they bring forth the
things we once chose to leave behind. And though they
have been here before, they make earth seem
like anything but a planet to be inhabited.

Recognize the character of this wilderness as winds
rip down our monuments and gutters become
choked with snow. What has come back may never
stifle the remarkable fertility of the ever-present.

A Similar Search

But the orchids grow readily in the real world too

Pleasure can be terrifying
when the immensity of its emptiness shows us what we don't know
so, confident in our mannerisms of bombast
we make and remake ourselves from such undesirable artifacts.

A wild tonic of devotion
warms our bones as we negotiate the pleats of some infinite rock face
where our hope, at least, is to fail the right way
and the end of safety is made apparent by the lack of summits.

Operatic in scope
we sink deep into the wounds of our beloved to create an unknown
    thing
and to listen for those singing into chaos
while the tyranny of thought forces them towards another world.

Reduced to language
the questions arise as to who is responsible for their homecoming, if
    anyone
and exercises in sentiment trundle to a halt
as we discover the clarion call, which enables their return.

"But the orchids grow readily in the real world too."

Acknowledgments

Many thanks to the individuals whose support, inspiration, and constant contact helped improve these poems considerably: Leighton and Donna Lindo, Mariana Bohlemann, Kimberly Kannal, Rusol Yasin, Stephanie Marsh, and Renee Golembiowski.

www.litotes208.com

CPSIA information can be obtained
at www.ICGtesting.com
Printed in the USA
BVHW031100261118
534009BV00004B/401/P

9 781387 909674